Women in Battle

150 YEARS OF FIGHTING FOR FREEDOM, EQUALITY AND SISTERHOOD

MARTA BREEN AND
JENNY JORDAHL

TRANSLATED BY SIÂN MACKIES

D1079126

FOREWORD

Women in Battle is a 150-year history of the fight for freedom, equality and sisterhood in a digestible and accessible form. It's a book to enjoy, to read and to share. This isn't a history of conventional war but of a very different type of battle. How have women worldwide fought to be heard, to be recognised and for the right to be able to realise their potential?

150 years ago the picture for women was stark. Unable to vote, to earn their own money, to access education, or to do what they wanted – whether inside or outside of the home – and unable to access contraception or abortion, women were systematically excluded from the workplace and decision-making processes, with black, disabled and gay women even further discriminated against.

Today we live in a different era. Women have spoken up and argued the case for equality: through the power of the pen and protest, the ideas of women, silenced for so long, have reshaped the world for the better. Women of all classes, races, backgrounds and countries have raised their voices and faced considerable jeopardy to do so.

This book tells the stories of women we should all know. From Lucretia Mott, the Quaker human rights activist; Harriet Tubman, the abolitionist activist born into slavery; Sojourner Truth, campaigning for the rights of black women to be heard within the suffrage movement; Olympe de Gouges, who wrote an alternative constitution to the *Declaration of the Rights of the Man* and was executed by guillotine; Mary Wollstonecraft, who penned *A Vindication of the Rights of Woman*; Táhirih, the Iranian poet martyred for her message of equality; to Malala, winner of the Nobel Peace Prize for her campaign for women's education.

These are women who used deeds and words to create opportunities
for people everywhere – men, women, boys and girls.
In the process they endured prison and persecution, risked their lives
and reputations – the fight for access to education, to end slavery,
to vote, for contraception and abortion, and for LGBTQI rights
didn't come easily. Yet today we do not know or celebrate these
heroic stories. All too often we fail to study these lives in university,
dramatise these histories in contemporary culture or record
the tales in history books.

It is urgent that we all learn more about the history of feminism.
It is the journey of our mothers, grandmothers and
great-grandmothers to where we are today. We stand on their
shoulders: the life I have led as a theatre-maker and artist was made
possible by their struggle and the struggle of millions of ordinary
women around the world who gave us the chance of a different life.

Women in Battle brings vividly to life the monumental achievements
of women around the world right up to the present day and paints
a picture of the ongoing struggles of half of humanity to be able to
reach our potential. Working with WOW – Women of the World –
festival across the globe, meeting activists from Karachi to Rio,
I am reminded that women still have barriers to bring down.
Although the last 150 years of history do give cause for optimism,
there is still so much to do – and maybe you could be part of the
next wave in the movement. This book is a wonderful guide
to the battle so far and to help you carry it on.

Jude Kelly
Founder of WOW – Women of the World festival

MEN AND WOMEN LIVED VERY DIFFERENT LIVES DURING THE 1800S.

WOMEN HAD FAR FEWER RIGHTS THAN MEN, THEY WERE NOT ALLOWED TO BE EDUCATED, AND THEY WERE NOT ALLOWED TO OWN LAND.

THIS MEANT THAT WOMEN WERE LARGELY UNABLE TO EARN THEIR OWN MONEY.

THEY WERE NOT ALLOWED TO VOTE IN ELECTIONS EITHER.

A WOMAN WAS INCAPACITATED, JUST LIKE A CHILD OR A SLAVE.

HER FATHER WOULD MAKE
DECISIONS FOR HER UNTIL SHE
WAS MARRIED.

THEN IT WAS HER
HUSBAND'S TURN.

WELL,
HERE
YOU GO!

WHEN THEY WERE MARRIED,
WOMEN HAD TO PROMISE TO
OBEY THEIR HUSBAND.

Women, be
submissive to
your husbands.

THE VERY FIRST MEETING

A MAJOR ANTI-SLAVERY CONFERENCE WAS ARRANGED IN ENGLAND IN 1840.

A DELEGATION OF BOTH MEN AND WOMEN CAME FROM THE USA. WHEN THE ORGANISERS FOUND OUT THAT WOMEN WERE TAKING PART, THERE WAS AN UPROAR.

WOMEN CAN'T TAKE PART IN POLITICAL MEETINGS

TUT, TUT!

BUT NOW THEY'RE HERE... WHAT CAN WE DO?

HM...

THE AMERICAN WOMEN WERE NOT ALLOWED TO SPEAK, AND HAD TO SIT QUIETLY AND LISTEN BEHIND A CURTAIN.

MANY OF THE WOMEN FOUND THIS UNFAIR.

THEY HAD WORKED TO ABOLISH SLAVERY FOR YEARS AND NOW THEY WERE BEING EXCLUDED.

WHO'S SPEAKING?

THIS!

A GUY...

GAH!

BAH!

ARE YOU THINKING WHAT I'M THINKING?

OH, YES! DEFINITELY!

ELIZABETH CADY STANTON
(1815–1902)

LUCRETIA MOTT
(1793–1880)

STANTON STARTED WRITING A DECLARATION ON EQUALITY. SHE BASED IT ON THE AMERICAN DECLARATION OF INDEPENDENCE FROM 1776.

and women
All men ⌄are created equal

SHE WROTE THAT GIRLS SHOULD HAVE THE RIGHT TO AN EDUCATION AND THAT WOMEN SHOULD BE ALLOWED TO MANAGE THEIR OWN INCOME AND HAVE THE RIGHT TO A DIVORCE.

MOTT AND STANTON WERE BOTH ABOLITIONISTS. THIS MOVEMENT PROMOTED HUMAN RIGHTS. THEY WANTED TO ABOLISH SLAVERY, CRUELTY TO ANIMALS, CUSTODIAL SENTENCES, PROSTITUTION AND THE OPPRESSION OF WOMEN.

DECLARATION — OF — SENTIMENTS

THE NEW DECLARATION WAS PRESENTED AT A CONFERENCE FOR ABOLITIONISTS IN SENECA FALLS, NEW YORK, IN 1848.

AROUND A HUNDRED WOMEN AND MEN SIGNED IT.

THIS ASSEMBLY IS CONSIDERED THE FIRST MEETING IN THE HISTORY OF THE WOMEN'S MOVEMENT.

WOMEN'S STRUGGLE AGAINST SLAVERY

HARRIET TUBMAN
(CIRCA 1822–1913)

DURING THE 1700S AND 1800S, AROUND HALF A MILLION AFRICANS WERE TAKEN TO AMERICA AS SLAVES.

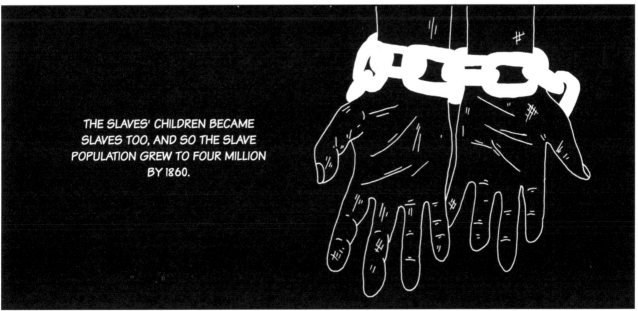

THE SLAVES' CHILDREN BECAME SLAVES TOO, AND SO THE SLAVE POPULATION GREW TO FOUR MILLION BY 1860.

THE SLAVES WERE FORCED TO WORK ON PLANTATIONS WHERE RICE, TOBACCO AND COTTON WERE GROWN.

MANY OF THEM WERE MISTREATED BY THE PLANTATION OWNERS.

SLAVES WHO TRIED TO ESCAPE WERE OFTEN KILLED.

HARRIET TUBMAN WAS BORN INTO SLAVERY.

WHEN SHE WAS SIX, SHE WAS TAKEN FROM HER PARENTS TO WORK ON A DIFFERENT PLANTATION.

HERE SHE WAS CONSTANTLY WHIPPED AND BEATEN.

ONE DAY AN IRON WEIGHT WAS THROWN AT HER HEAD.

THUMP

SHE WAS UNCONSCIOUS FOR TWO DAYS.

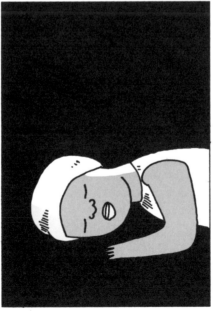

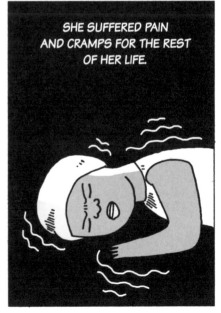

SHE SUFFERED PAIN AND CRAMPS FOR THE REST OF HER LIFE.

WHEN SHE WAS 27, HARRIET MANAGED TO ESCAPE FROM THE PLANTATION.

SHE MADE IT TO PHILADELPHIA, WHERE SLAVERY WAS FORBIDDEN.

WOW!

LIKE ARRIVING IN HEAVEN!

BUT SHE COULDN'T ENJOY HER FREEDOM.

SHE WANTED TO HELP OTHER SLAVES TO ESCAPE.

BACK I GO!

HARRIET THOUGHT UP ESCAPE PLANS AND ROUTES.

THE ESCAPES WERE MADE IN SECRET AT NIGHT.

HARRIET LED SEVERAL HUNDRED SLAVES TO FREEDOM.

CARRY ON OR DIE!

IF THE SLAVES PANICKED AND WANTED TO GO BACK TO THE PLANTATION, SHE THREATENED TO SHOOT THEM.

A SUBSTANTIAL REWARD WAS OFFERED FOR THE PERSON WHO COULD CAPTURE HER.

BUT NO ONE COULD.

THE NOVEL "UNCLE TOM'S CABIN", WRITTEN BY HARRIET BEECHER STOWE, WAS PUBLISHED IN 1852. THE BOOK WAS ABOUT SLAVERY IN THE USA – FROM THE SLAVES' PERSPECTIVE.

THE NOVEL GARNERED A LOT OF ATTENTION AND WAS THE BESTSELLING BOOK AFTER THE BIBLE DURING THE 1800S.

HMPH!

BESTSELLERS

"UNCLE TOM'S CABIN" REALLY HELPED INCREASE OPPOSITION TO SLAVERY.

APPALLING!

IT JUST CAN'T BE!

NO, THIS CAN'T GO ON!

IN MARCH 1861, ABRAHAM LINCOLN WAS ELECTED PRESIDENT OF THE USA. HE WANTED TO ABOLISH SLAVERY.

THERE WERE LARGE PLANTATIONS RUN BY SLAVES IN THE SOUTH. THESE STATES PROTESTED AND DEMANDED THEIR INDEPENDENCE.

WE'LL BE OUR OWN NATION.

THIS MARKED THE START OF A BLOODY CIVIL WAR.

620,000 SOLDIERS AND AN UNKNOWN NUMBER OF CIVILIANS WERE KILLED BEFORE LINCOLN AND THE NORTHERN STATES WON.

WE WON!

SO YOU'RE THE LITTLE LADY WHO STARTED THIS TERRIBLE WAR?

WHEN THE CIVIL WAR WAS OVER, BLACK MEN WERE GIVEN THE RIGHT TO VOTE. WOMEN WERE STILL EXCLUDED FROM POLITICS.

IN 1869, ELIZABETH CADY STANTON STARTED THE FIRST AMERICAN ASSOCIATION FOR WOMEN'S SUFFRAGE, TOGETHER WITH TEACHER SUSAN B. ANTHONY.

HARRIET TUBMAN WAS ALSO INVOLVED IN THE WORK.

THERE WERE BOUND TO BE LINKS BETWEEN THE SUFFRAGE MOVEMENT AND THE ANTI-SLAVERY MOVEMENT, SINCE BOTH WOMEN AND BLACK PEOPLE WERE INCAPACITATED IN SOCIETY.

ANOTHER FORMER SLAVE WHO MADE HER MARK ON FEMINISM WAS SOJOURNER TRUTH.

SOJOURNER TRUTH
(CA. 1797–1883)

SHE GREW UP ON A SLAVE PLANTATION IN NEW YORK.

AS AN ADULT, TRUTH HAD A SON AND A DAUGHTER.

JUST AFTER HER DAUGHTER WAS BORN, SHE MANAGED TO ESCAPE WITH HER.

SHE WENT TO COURT TO GET HER SON BACK FROM THE SLAVE OWNER.

TRUTH WAS THE FIRST BLACK WOMAN TO WIN SUCH A CASE AGAINST A WHITE MAN.

AT THE AGE OF 70, SHE GAVE A FAMOUS SPEECH AT A WOMEN'S RIGHTS MEETING.

MY FRIENDS!

HER SPEECH WAS AIMED AT THOSE FIGHTING FOR THE SUFFRAGE OF WHITE WOMEN WITHOUT REALISING THAT BLACK WOMEN HAD NO RIGHTS AT ALL.

THERE IS A GREAT STIR ABOUT BLACK MEN GETTING THEIR RIGHTS.

BUT NOT A WORD ABOUT THE BLACK WOMEN.

IF BLACK MEN GET THEIR RIGHTS AND NOT BLACK WOMEN THEIRS...

...YOU SEE THE MEN WILL BE MASTERS OVER THE WOMEN...

AND IT WILL BE JUST AS BAD AS IT WAS BEFORE.

IN THE YEARS FOLLOWING THE
FIRST WOMEN'S RIGHTS MEETING,
FEMINIST GROUPS EMERGED ALL
OVER THE WESTERN WORLD.

THE THREE MOST IMPORTANT CAUSES THE WOMEN'S MOVEMENT HAS FOUGHT FOR ARE:

THE RIGHT TO RECEIVE AN EDUCATION, GET A JOB AND EARN ONE'S OWN MONEY

THE RIGHT TO VOTE IN POLITICAL ELECTIONS

THE RIGHT TO BODILY INTEGRITY

BIOLOGY WAS USED TO JUSTIFY THIS: IT WAS NOT IN A WOMAN'S NATURE TO USE HER HEAD.

SO I WAS THINKING...

THINKING?!? HOW UNNATURAL!

AS WAS RELIGION: THIS WAS WHAT GOD HAD INTENDED.

THAT'S HOW YOU WANT IT, RIGHT, GOD?

HELLO?

I'LL TAKE THAT AS A "YES".

THE LATE 1600S SAW THE ADVENT OF THE

ENLIGHTENMENT

IN EUROPE.

HM...

SCIENCE MADE GREAT PROGRESS.

BOINK!

GRAVITY!!

THIS RESULTED IN THE CHURCH LOSING SOME OF ITS POWER OVER SOCIETY.

GOD CONTROLS EVERYTHING!

YEAH? THEN WHAT ABOUT THE LAWS OF NATURE?

PEOPLE WERE GIVEN NEW AND MORE CREDIBLE EXPLANATIONS THAN THOSE OFFERED BY CHRISTIANITY.

WE ARE THE CENTRE!

THE SUN'S THE CENTRE!

ONE OF THE ERA'S LEADING THINKERS WAS THE PHILOSOPHER ROUSSEAU.

HIS IDEAS ABOUT HUMAN RIGHTS AND DEMOCRACY INSPIRED THE FRENCH REVOLUTION IN 1789.

JEAN-JACQUES ROUSSEAU
(1712–1778)

HE HAD RADICAL THOUGHTS ABOUT EDUCATION. IN HIS TREATISE "EMILE" HE ARGUED AGAINST THE AUTHORITARIAN SCHOOLS OF THE ERA.

AHEM!

HE ALSO WRITES THAT IT IS IMPORTANT TO RAISE GIRLS AND BOYS DIFFERENTLY SINCE WOMEN AND MEN ARE FUNDAMENTALLY DIFFERENT.

THE GENDERS ARE COMPLEMENTARY. ONE SHOULD BE STRONG AND ACTIVE, THE OTHER WEAK AND PASSIVE. WOMEN REPRESENT SENSITIVITY AND MEN REASON.

ACCORDING TO ROUSSEAU, GIRLS SHOULD BE PREPARED FOR THEIR MOST IMPORTANT ROLE IN LIFE: SUPPORTING MEN.

TO PLEASE THEM, TO BE USEFUL TO THEM, TO MAKE THEMSELVES LOVED AND HONOURED BY THEM, TO EDUCATE THEM WHEN YOUNG, TO CARE FOR THEM WHEN GROWN, TO COUNCIL THEM, TO CONSOLE THEM, TO MAKE LIFE AGREEABLE TO THEM...

...THESE ARE THE DUTIES OF WOMEN AT ALL TIMES, AND SHOULD BE TAUGHT THEM FROM THEIR INFANCY!

RENOWNED GERMAN PHILOSOPHERS KANT AND HEGEL AGREED ENTIRELY WITH ROUSSEAU ON THE TOPIC OF THE INFERIORITY OF WOMEN.

AGREED!

LUCKILY THERE WERE ALSO FEMALE THINKERS...

OLYMPE DE GOUGES
(1748–1793)

MARY WOLLSTONECRAFT
(1759–1797)

BROS!

LIBERTY, EQUALITY, FRATERNITY

FRANCE ADOPTED ITS CONSTITUTION, THE "DECLARATION OF THE RIGHTS OF MAN AND OF THE CITIZEN", DURING THE FRENCH REVOLUTION. IT HAD A LOT TO SAY ABOUT "LIBERTY, EQUALITY AND FRATERNITY".

UNFORTUNATELY THESE NEW RIGHTS ONLY APPLIED TO MEN.

AUTHOR AND FEMINIST OLYMPE DE GOUGES WAS FURIOUS. IN 1791 SHE WROTE AN ALTERNATIVE CONSTITUTION.

DECLARATION OF THE RIGHTS OF WOMAN AND THE FEMALE CITIZEN

WOMAN HAS THE RIGHT TO MOUNT THE SCAFFOLD, SO SHE SHOULD EQUALLY HAVE THE RIGHT TO MOUNT THE ROSTRUM!

UNFORTUNATELY HER FAMOUS WORDS BECAME A SELF-FULFILLING PROPHECY:

OLYMPE WAS BEHEADED ON THE SCAFFOLD FOR HER OPPOSITION OF THE REVOLUTION'S VIOLENT LEADERS.

LUCKILY A BRITISH AUTHOR AND PHILOSOPHER – MARY WOLLSTONECRAFT – CONTINUED THE FIGHT ALONG THE SAME LINES.

WOLLSTONECRAFT WAS RUNNING A GIRLS' SCHOOL IN LONDON WHEN SHE WROTE HER FIRST BOOK, "THOUGHTS ON THE EDUCATION OF DAUGHTERS" (1787).

FIVE YEARS LATER CAME HER CLASSIC WORK "A VINDICATION OF THE RIGHTS OF WOMEN".

HERE SHE ATTACKED ROUSSEAU AND HIS VIEW OF "THE NATURE OF WOMEN".

IDIOT!

WOMEN ARE MORE INTERESTED IN BEAUTY AND EMBROIDERY BECAUSE THAT IS HOW THEY WERE RAISED.

EQUAL EDUCATION FOR GIRLS AND BOYS WOULD BENEFIT ALL OF SOCIETY. WELL-EDUCATED WOMEN WOULD BE MORE USEFUL MEMBERS OF SOCIETY...

...AND ALSO MORE INTERESTING CONVERSATION PARTNERS FOR THEIR HUSBANDS.

FROM THE END OF THE 1800S, WOMEN'S ORGANISATIONS ALL OVER THE WORLD WORKED TO GIVE WOMEN ACCESS TO EDUCATION AND WORK.

MORE AND MORE PROFESSIONS WERE OPENED UP TO WOMEN.

THE FEMALE WORKERS WERE OFTEN AT THE BOTTOM OF THE LADDER. THEY EARNED LESS AND HAD FEWER RIGHTS THAN THEIR MALE COLLEAGUES.

THE PRESSURE TO GIVE WOMEN THE RIGHT
TO VOTE INCREASED FROM THE LATE 1880S.
ASSOCIATIONS FIGHTING FOR THIS WERE
FORMED IN MANY COUNTRIES.

LEADING FEMINISTS FROM VARIOUS COUNTRIES
TRAVELLED TO CONFERENCES AND VISITED EACH
OTHER. AN INTERNATIONAL NETWORK EMERGED.

VOTES FOR WOMEN

RÖSTRÄTT FÖR KVINNOR

FRAUENSTIMMRECHT JA!

VOTO PARA LA MUJER

STEMMERETT FOR KVINNER NÅ!

LES FEMMES FRANÇAISES VEULENT VOTER

MILLICENT FAWCETT
(1847–1929)

EMMELINE PANKHURST
(1858–1928)

THE UNITED KINGDOM HAD THE MOST ACTIVE MOVEMENT. AUTHOR AND FEMINIST MILLICENT FAWCETT WORKED ACTIVELY TO INFLUENCE THE COUNTRY'S POLITICIANS.

IN 1897 SHE FOUNDED THE FIRST UNION OF WOMEN'S SUFFRAGE SOCIETIES.

NATIONAL UNION OF WOMEN'S SUFFRAGE SOCIETIES

BUT CONVINCING THE BRITISH POLITICIANS PROVED MORE DIFFICULT THAN YOU WOULD THINK.

THE MAJOR PARTIES DISMISSED THE CAUSE AGAIN AND AGAIN.

SUFFRAGE FOR WOMEN WAS NOT CONSIDERED AN IMPORTANT MATTER.

EHHH, NO.

THERE WAS ALSO A STRONG COUNTERMOVEMENT ARGUING THAT POLITICS WERE SIMPLY NOT IN A WOMAN'S NATURE.

WOMEN SHOULD BE AT HOME WITH THEIR FAMILIES AND SHOULDN'T WORRY ABOUT ANYTHING ELSE.

PRECISELY!

AS THE YEARS PASSED, THE FEMINISTS GREW MORE IMPATIENT.

ENOUGH IS ENOUGH.

HOUSEWIFE EMMELINE PANKHURST WAS THE MOST IMPATIENT OF ALL. SINCE A MODERATE APPROACH WAS NOT WORKING, SHE THOUGHT IT WAS TIME FOR A MILITANT APPROACH.

SHE FORMED A NEW UNION, THE MEMBERS OF WHICH SOON BECAME KNOWN AS THE SUFFRAGETTES.

WOMENS SOCIAL AND POLITICAL UNION

HER DAUGHTERS, SYLVIA, CHRISTABEL AND ADELA, WERE ALSO LINKED TO THE MOVEMENT.

SYLVIA

CHRISTABEL

ADELA

MANY SUFFRAGETTES WERE RADICAL WOMEN FROM THE UPPER CLASS. THEY WERE ABLE TO SPEND TIME ON POLITICAL WORK. BUT TEACHERS, NURSES AND FACTORY WORKERS ALSO PARTICIPATED IN THE MOVEMENT.

ACTION NOT WORDS

DURING 1912 AND 1913 THE SUFFRAGETTES WERE RESPONSIBLE FOR SEVERAL HUNDRED BOMBINGS AND FIRES.

THEY CHAINED THEMSELVES TO RAILINGS, SET FIRE TO LETTER BOXES AND BROKE SHOP WINDOWS TO GET THEIR MESSAGE ACROSS.

POST

POST

PEOPLE WERE VERY SHOCKED THAT WOMEN COULD DO SUCH THINGS.

IT'S THE WOMEN...

GOOD GOD!

PUBLIC PLACES THAT WERE ONLY OPEN TO MEN WERE PARTICULARLY SUSCEPTIBLE TO ATTACK.

MOST GOLF CLUBS DID NOT ALLOW WOMEN TO PLAY.

WHEN THE GOLF SEASON STARTED IN 1918, THE MEN WERE MET WITH THIS SIGHT:

NO SUFFRAGE, NO GOLF

AMONG THE SUFFRAGETTES' MOST
FAMOUS ACTIONS WAS THE BOMBING
OF FUTURE PRIME MINISTER DAVID LLOYD
GEORGE'S HOUSE...

...AND THEN SUFFRAGETTE EMILY DAVISON THREW HERSELF IN FRONT OF KING GEORGE V'S HORSE DURING A RACE ON 4 JULY 1913.

EMILY WAS TRAMPLED AND DIED FROM HER INJURIES.

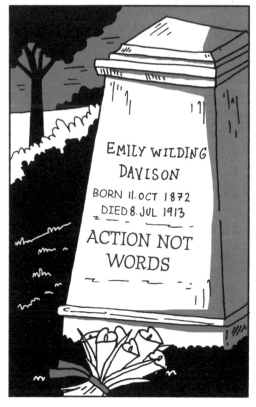

EMILY WILDING DAVISON

BORN 11. OCT 1872
DIED 8. JUL 1913

ACTION NOT WORDS

MANY FEMINISTS DISTANCED THEMSELVES FROM THE SUFFRAGETTES AND THEIR ACTIONS.

PIONEER MILLICENT FAWCETT WAS AMONG THEM.

VIOLENCE WILL ONLY CONVINCE MEN THAT WOMEN ARE NOT READY FOR SUFFRAGE.

THE SUFFRAGETTES DID NOT WANT TO HARM ANYONE. THEIR ACTIONS WERE CARRIED OUT WHEN THE BUILDINGS WERE EMPTY.

THE FIGHT WAS HARDEST ON THE SUFFRAGETTES THEMSELVES. THEY WERE ARRESTED AND BEATEN BY THE POLICE AGAIN AND AGAIN.

EMMELINE PANKHURST – LIKE HUNDREDS OF HER FELLOW WOMEN – WAS IMPRISONED SEVERAL TIMES.

WHEN THE AUTHORITIES WOULD NOT RECOGNISE THE SUFFRAGETTES AS POLITICAL PRISONERS, THEY DECIDED TO GO ON A HUNGER STRIKE.

THE POLICE RESPONDED BY FORCE-FEEDING THEM.

THIS TREATMENT WAS PAINFUL AND DANGEROUS TO THEIR HEALTH. SEVERAL OF THEM DEVELOPED PNEUMONIA AND OTHER LIFE-THREATENING ILLNESSES.

THAT IS WHY THE POLITICIANS INTRODUCED THE "CAT AND MOUSE ACT":

THE MOST EMACIATED HUNGER STRIKERS WERE RELEASED. WHEN THEY WERE HEALTHY AGAIN, THEY WENT STRAIGHT BACK TO PRISON.

OUT!!

VOTES FOR WOMEN

WELCOME BACK.

WHEN THE FIRST WORLD WAR BROKE OUT IN 1914, THE SUFFRAGETTES PUT THEIR FIGHT ON HOLD. THEY NOW PUT ALL THEIR ENERGY INTO FIGHTING FOR THEIR COUNTRY. MANY OF THEM SIGNED UP FOR VOLUNTARY DUTY.

THE GOVERNMENT RELEASED ALL THE FEMINISTS IN PRISON.

WE NEED YOU.

WHEN THE MEN WENT TO WAR, WOMEN TOOK OVER MUCH OF THE DAY-TO-DAY WORK IN THE COUNTRY. MANY ALSO WORKED IN THE FIELD AS NURSES AND PARAMEDICS.

WHEN THE WAR WAS OVER, ATTITUDES TO WOMEN'S SUFFRAGE HAD CHANGED.

SO, ABOUT SUFFRAGE...?

UM...

THE POLITICIANS HAD SEEN WITH THEIR OWN EYES THAT WOMEN COULD COPE OUTSIDE THEIR KITCHENS.

YOU WERE RIGHT.

AND?

WE WERE WRONG.

YUP!

IN 1918 BRITISH WOMEN OVER THE AGE OF 30 WERE GIVEN THE RIGHT TO VOTE.

MEN OVER THE AGE OF 21 HAD THE RIGHT TO VOTE, BUT WOMEN THAT YOUNG WERE CONSIDERED TOO "SCATTERBRAINED".

STOP RIGHT THERE! YOU'RE TOO YOUNG AND SCATTERBRAINED!

TEN YEARS LATER – A FEW MONTHS BEFORE EMMELINE PANKHURST DIED – THIS RIGHT WAS GIVEN TO ALL WOMEN OVER THE AGE OF 21.

EMMELINE!!

WE WON!

THE FIRST COUNTRY IN THE WORLD TO GIVE WOMEN THE RIGHT TO VOTE WITH NO RESTRICTIONS WAS NEW ZEALAND. FINLAND WAS THE FIRST COUNTRY IN EUROPE.

SPAIN 1931

FRANCE 1944

ITALY 1946

ISRAEL 1948

GREECE 1952

UNITED KINGDOM 1928

SWEDEN 1921

USA 1920

GERMANY 1918

SOVIET UNION 1917

THE IRANIAN MARTYR

THE FIRST KNOWN MARTYR OF THE WOMEN'S MOVEMENT WAS NOT BRITISH, BUT IRANIAN.

SHE WAS A POET CALLED TÁHIRIH.

TÁHIRIH
(BORN BETWEEN 1814 AND 1817, DIED IN 1852)

TÁHIRIH GREW UP IN A HIGHLY RESPECTED FAMILY. HER FATHER WAS A MULLAH.

GIRLS WERE NOT ALLOWED TO BE EDUCATED, BUT SHE FOLLOWED HER FATHER'S TEACHINGS IN SECRET.

TÁHIRIH WAS EXTREMELY TALENTED AND INTELLIGENT.

HER MOTHER DESPAIRED AND SAID SHE SHOULD BEHAVE LIKE HER SISTERS.

YOU DON'T NEED THAT KNOWLEDGE. MAKE YOURSELF USEFUL INSTEAD!

53

AT THE AGE OF 14 SHE WAS MARRIED TO A COUSIN SHE DIDN'T LIKE.

STOP THAT!

A FEW YEARS LATER SHE CONVERTED TO THE BÁBÍ FAITH.

IN THIS RELIGION, MEN AND WOMEN ARE EQUAL.

HER HUSBAND DEMANDED A DIVORCE AND DENIED HER ACCESS TO THEIR THREE CHILDREN.

EVEN THOUGH WOMEN WERE FORBIDDEN FROM SPEAKING IN PUBLIC, TÁHIRIH NOW SPENT ALL HER TIME SPREADING HER MESSAGE OF EQUALITY.

SHE ONCE REMOVED HER VEIL IN FRONT OF A GROUP OF MEN AT A RELIGIOUS MEETING.

AM I NOT YOUR SISTER? ARE YOU NOT MY BROTHERS? CAN'T YOU CONSIDER ME A FRIEND — ONE OF YOU?

THIS INCIDENT LED TO HER ARREST. SHE WAS PLACED UNDER HOUSE ARREST IN TEHERAN FOR MANY YEARS.

YOU CAN KILL ME AT ANY TIME, BUT YOU CAN'T STOP THE LIBERATION OF WOMEN!

IN 1852 TÁHIRIH WAS SENTENCED TO DEATH.

SHE WAS STRANGLED WITH HER OWN VEIL AND THROWN INTO A WELL.

NOT EVERYONE LIKED WOMEN HAVING JOBS.

NOW THE WOMEN CAN STEAL OUR JOBS!

MANY WOMEN FOUND THEY WERE EXCLUDED IN THE WORKPLACE.

THEY WERE OFTEN SUBJECT TO SEXUAL HARASSMENT AND ASSAULT.

THE FEMALE WORKERS WERE TREATED WORSE THAN THE MEN.

THEY WERE PAID LESS THAN MEN...

...AND THEY WERE OFTEN FIRED FIRST.

YOUR HUSBAND CAN LOOK AFTER YOU!

UNTIL NOW THE WOMEN'S MOVEMENT HAD BEEN DOMINATED BY MIDDLE-CLASS WOMEN.

AT THE BEGINNING OF THE 1900S WORKING-CLASS WOMEN ALSO STARTED TO MOBILISE.

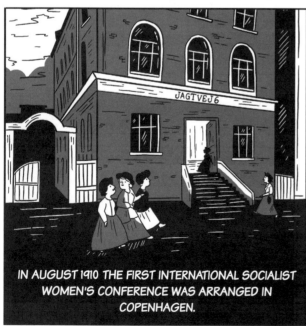

IN AUGUST 1910 THE FIRST INTERNATIONAL SOCIALIST WOMEN'S CONFERENCE WAS ARRANGED IN COPENHAGEN.

THE SOCIALISTS CONSIDERED THE WOMEN'S MOVEMENT PART OF THE CLASS STRUGGLE.

RENOWNED GERMAN FEMINIST CLARA ZETKIN WAS AMONG THE 130 WOMEN WHO PARTICIPATED.

WORKERS ARE BEING EXPLOITED AND OPPRESSED IN EVERY COUNTRY. WE HAVE MUTUAL INTERESTS AND MUST UNITE!

FEMALE WORKERS ARE DOUBLY OPPRESSED! BY BOTH CAPITALIST EMPLOYERS AND MEN.

WE NEED AN ANNUAL INTERNATIONAL WOMEN'S DAY TO FOCUS ON THE RIGHTS OF FEMALE WORKERS.

AND SO THE IDEA FOR 8 MARCH CAME ABOUT.

THE FOLLOWING YEAR, IN 1911, THIS WOMEN'S DAY WAS
MARKED IN DENMARK, GERMANY, AUSTRIA, SWITZERLAND
AND THE USA. MORE THAN A MILLION WOMEN PARTICIPATED.

WHEN THE FIRST WORLD WAR BROKE OUT, THE INTERNATIONAL LABOUR MOVEMENT WAS DIVIDED.

IT WAS DIFFICULT TO MAINTAIN SOLIDARITY WHEN THE COUNTRIES WERE AT WAR WITH EACH OTHER.

PACIFISM WAS STRONG AMONG THE WOMEN. BOTH CLARA ZETKIN AND HER GOOD FRIEND ROSA LUXEMBURG WERE ANTI-WAR.

THE WORKERS HAVE NOTHING TO GAIN FROM THIS WAR. THEY RISK LOSING EVERYTHING THEY HOLD DEAR.

THEY THOUGHT THAT THE WAR ONLY SERVED THE CAPITALISTS: THOSE PRODUCING WEAPONS AND CANONS, WARSHIPS AND AMMUNITION.

WHEN THE GERMAN WORKERS' PARTY BACKED THE AUTHORITIES' WARFARE, CLARA AND ROSA LEFT THE PARTY.

BYE NOW!

THEY STARTED A COMMUNIST PEACE MOVEMENT.

BOTH OF THEM WERE ARRESTED SEVERAL TIMES FOR INCITING MEN TO REFUSE CONSCRIPTION.

"WHEN MEN KILL, WE WOMEN MUST FIGHT TO PRESERVE LIFE. WHEN MEN ARE SILENT, WE MUST RAISE OUR VOICES."

IN JANUARY 1919 ROSA LUXEMBURG AND COMRADE KARL LIEBKNECHT WERE ARRESTED BY THE RIGHT-WING SOLDIERS IN BERLIN.

THEY WERE BOTH SHOT.

CLARA ZETKIN CONTINUED HER FIGHT FOR PEACE AND SOCIALISM UNTIL SHE DIED IN RUSSIA, AGED 76, ON THE RUN FROM THE NAZIS.

SHE IS BURIED IN RED SQUARE.

MARGARET SANGER
(1879–1966)

THE STRUGGLE FOR FEMALE BODILY INTEGRITY

NO WOMEN CAN CALL HERSELF FREE WHO DOES NOT OWN AND CONTROL HER BODY.

IN THE PAST FAMILIES OFTEN HAD MANY CHILDREN, PARTICULARLY POOR FAMILIES.

THERE WAS NO CONTRACEPTION AND NOWHERE TO GET AN ABORTION.

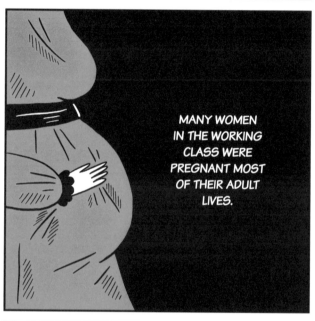

MANY WOMEN IN THE WORKING CLASS WERE PREGNANT MOST OF THEIR ADULT LIVES.

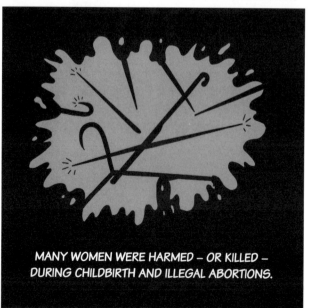

MANY WOMEN WERE HARMED – OR KILLED – DURING CHILDBIRTH AND ILLEGAL ABORTIONS.

THIS WORRIED AMERICAN NURSE MARGARET SANGER, WHO LIVED IN NEW YORK IN THE EARLY 1900S.

HER OWN MOTHER DIED YOUNG AFTER BEING PREGNANT 18 TIMES. ONLY 11 OF MARGARET'S SIBLINGS SURVIVED BIRTH.

AS A NURSE IN ONE OF THE CITY'S WORKING-CLASS AREAS, SHE SAW HOW MANY WOMEN SUFFERED SIMILAR FATES.

SHE STARTED TEACHING PEOPLE HOW TO AVOID BECOMING PREGNANT.

THIS IS A "DOUCHEBAG".

A PUMP THAT WILL RINSE SPERM FROM YOUR VAGINA.

THERE WAS A GREAT NEED FOR SUCH INFORMATION. THERE WAS NO SEXUAL EDUCATION AT SCHOOL AND DOCTORS WERE SILENT ON THE SUBJECT.

TEACHING PEOPLE ABOUT CONTRACEPTION WAS FORBIDDEN. IT WAS CONSIDERED IMMORAL.

CONTRACEPTION!

MARGARET STARTED ISSUING HER OWN PAMPHLET, "THE WOMAN REBEL".

HERE SHE WROTE ABOUT SEXUALITY IN AN UNCOMMONLY OPEN WAY. THIS ANGERED AND SHOCKED SOME READERS.

FOR OTHERS IT WAS LIBERATING TO READ SUCH FRANK TEXTS ON A TABOO TOPIC.

MARGARET WAS ACCUSED OF "DISTRIBUTING OBSCENE MATERIAL".

TO ESCAPE A YEAR IN PRISON, SHE FLED TO EUROPE.

SOME EUROPEAN COUNTRIES HAD A MORE LIBERAL OPINION OF CONTRACEPTION. WHEN MARGARET VISITED A DUTCH WOMEN'S CLINIC IN 1915, SHE LEARNED ABOUT DIAPHRAGMS.

A DIAPHRAGM IS A KIND OF RUBBER DOME THAT IS INSERTED INTO THE VAGINA BEFORE SEX.

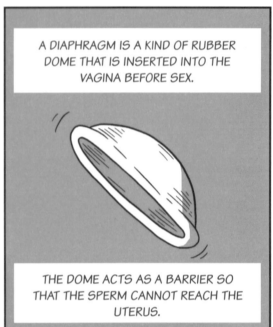

THE DOME ACTS AS A BARRIER SO THAT THE SPERM CANNOT REACH THE UTERUS.

FOR CENTURIES PEOPLE HAD EXPERIMENTED WITH DIFFERENT METHODS OF BARRING THE SPERM FROM THE UTERUS.

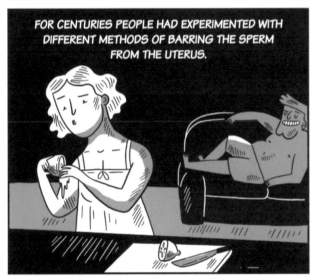

IT WAS ONLY WHEN MODERN RUBBER TECHNOLOGY BECAME AVAILABLE IN THE LATE 1800S THAT DIAPHRAGMS STARTED BEING PRODUCED.

MARGARET DECIDED TO IMPORT THEM ILLEGALLY TO THE USA.

BACK HOME, SHE OPENED THE USA'S FIRST WOMEN'S CLINIC TOGETHER WITH HER LITTLE SISTER, ETHEL.

46 AMBOY STREET

THE CLINIC WAS ONLY OPEN FOR TEN DAYS BEFORE THE SISTERS WERE ARRESTED.

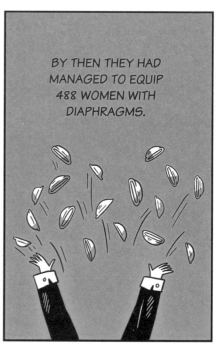

BY THEN THEY HAD MANAGED TO EQUIP 488 WOMEN WITH DIAPHRAGMS.

MARGARET AND ETHEL HAD TO SPEND 30 DAYS IN PRISON.

THEIR ARRESTS DID NOT GO UNNOTICED. MORE AND MORE PEOPLE SIDED WITH THEM.

THE AUTHORITIES FINALLY RELENTED. DOCTORS WERE ALLOWED TO GIVE ADVICE ON CONTRACEPTION – AND IN SOME CASES TO DISTRIBUTE IT.

MARGARET CONTINUED TO SPREAD HER MESSAGE INTERNATIONALLY. SHE LED CAMPAIGNS FOR FAMILY PLANNING IN INDIA AND JAPAN, AMONG OTHER THINGS.

THE ZEITGEIST WAS ON HER SIDE: SOCIAL REFORMS, HYGIENE AND MODERN MEDICINE LED TO LOWER INFANT MORTALITY IN LARGE PARTS OF THE WORLD.

THERE WAS NO LONG A NEED TO "SAFEGUARD" BY HAVING MANY CHILDREN. AND WITH FEWER MOUTHS TO FEED, FAMILIES' FINANCES IMPROVED.

MARGARET ALWAYS DREAMED OF MORE EFFECTIVE CONTRACEPTION.

WHAT ABOUT A HORMONE PILL?

IN THE EARLY 1950S SHE RECRUITED RESEARCHER GREGORY PINCUS.

HMM...

HMM...

AH-HAH!

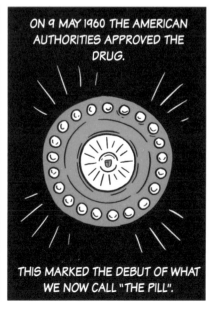

ON 9 MAY 1960 THE AMERICAN AUTHORITIES APPROVED THE DRUG.

THIS MARKED THE DEBUT OF WHAT WE NOW CALL "THE PILL".

THE PILL WAS ESSENTIAL TO "THE SEXUAL REVOLUTION" OF THE 1960S.

NOW SEX WAS LESS TO DO WITH HAVING CHILDREN, BUT WAS INSTEAD CONSIDERED A SOURCE OF JOY FOR BOTH MEN AND WOMEN.

NO MORE KNITTING NEEDLES, WISE WOMEN, PAINFUL MEMORIES!

FOR MOST OF THE 1900S ABORTION WAS STRICTLY FORBIDDEN IN MOST COUNTRIES OF THE WORLD.

IT DIDN'T MATTER IF YOU HAD MORE CHILDREN THAN YOU COULD FEED...

...OR IF YOU HAD BEEN RAPED.

HAVING CHILDREN OUT OF WEDLOCK WAS SHAMEFUL.

"ILLEGITIMATE" CHILDREN HAD FAR FEWER RIGHTS IN SOCIETY. SINGLE MOTHERS LIVED IN ABJECT POVERTY.

IT THEREFORE WAS NOT UNCOMMON FOR WOMEN TO ATTEMPT ABORTIONS ON THEIR OWN.

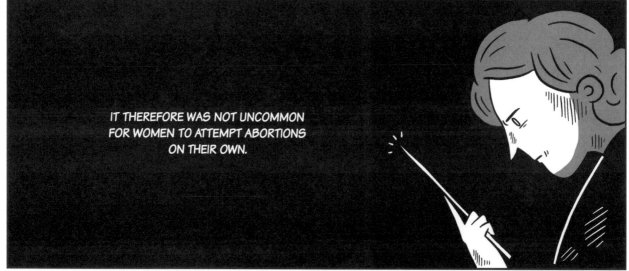

SOME VISITED ILLEGAL CLINICS

OR "WISE WOMEN".

OTHERS MADE DESPERATE ATTEMPTS USING KNITTING NEEDLES...

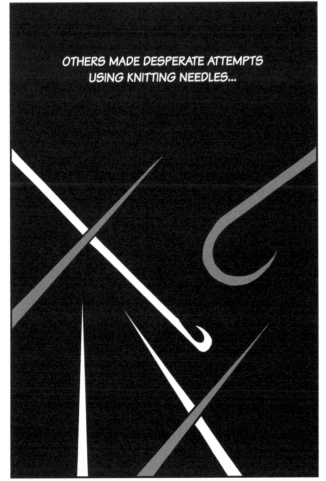

...OR BY "FALLING".

IN SOME WESTERN COUNTRIES ABORTION WAS PERMITTED IN EXCEPTIONAL CASES. YOU WOULD BE BROUGHT BEFORE A COMMITTEE TO EXPLAIN WHY YOU WANTED AN ABORTION.

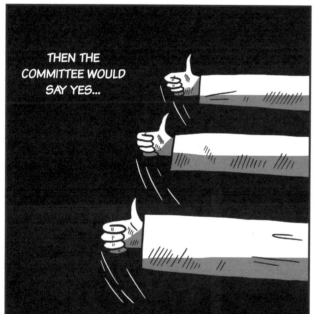

THEN THE COMMITTEE WOULD SAY YES...

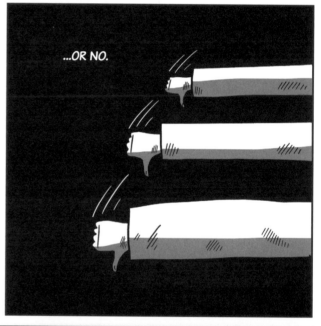

...OR NO.

IN 1973 A NEW LAW GAVE WOMEN IN THE USA THE RIGHT TO CHOOSE WHETHER THEY WANTED AN ABORTION.

THE CASE BEGAN WHEN 21-YEAR-OLD NORMA MCCORVEY FROM DALLAS IN TEXAS FELL PREGNANT WITH HER THIRD CHILD.

SHE LIVED A HARD LIFE AS A DRUG ADDICT, AND HER FIRST TWO CHILDREN WERE GIVEN UP FOR ADOPTION.

IN TEXAS, ABORTION WAS ONLY ALLOWED IF THE MOTHER'S LIFE WAS IN DANGER.

SHE CONTACTED A LAWYER TO ARRANGE THE ADOPTION.

HENRY McCULSKEY

HE PUT HER IN TOUCH WITH TWO OTHER LAWYERS WHO WERE LOOKING FOR A CASE THAT MIGHT CHALLENGE THE STRICT ABORTION LAW.

ARE YOU WILLING TO TAKE YOUR CASE TO THE SUPREME COURT?

YES!

WHEN NORMA WON HER CASE, THE STATE OF TEXAS APPEALED TO THE US SUPREME COURT.

THE SUPREME COURT JUDGED THE BAN TO BE UNCONSTITUTIONAL. AFTER THIS, EVERY US STATE HAD TO ALLOW ABORTION.

THE JUDGMENT FROM 1973 GARNERED A LOT OF ATTENTION WORLDWIDE. IN THE YEARS THAT FOLLOWED, PEOPLE FOUGHT FOR THIS RIGHT IN A NUMBER OF OTHER WESTERN COUNTRIES.

BUT THE DEBATE CONTINUES. THE AMERICAN PEOPLE ARE DIVIDED AND MANY ARE OPPOSING THE LAW IN ANY WAY POSSIBLE.

IN 1976 THE FIRST ABORTION CLINIC IN THE USA WAS TORCHED.

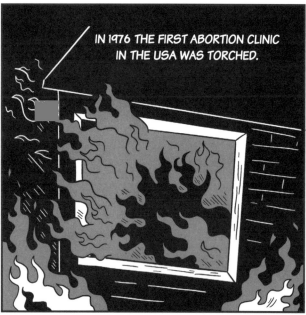

SUBSEQUENTLY A NUMBER OF OTHER CLINICS WERE BOMBED.

EIGHT MEMBERS OF STAFF ARE KILLED AND ATTEMPTS ARE MADE TO KILL TENS OF OTHERS.

WE TRADITIONALLY TALK ABOUT WAVES IN THE HISTORY OF FEMINISM. THE FIRST WAVE WAS THE ACTIVISM FOR WOMEN'S RIGHT TO VOTE, IN THE LATE 19TH CENTURY.

THE WOMEN'S MOVEMENT IN THE 1970S IS CONSIDERED THE SECOND WAVE. THE THIRD WAVE CAME DURING THE 1990S, WITH AN INCREASED FOCUS ON DIVERSITY AND INDIVIDUAL FREEDOM.

THE VENUS SYMBOL – WITH A CLENCHED FIST
IN THE MIDDLE – BECAME THE SYMBOL OF THE
WOMEN'S MOVEMENT DURING THE 1970S.

THE UN DENOTED 1975 INTERNATIONAL WOMEN'S YEAR. THE HIGHLIGHT WAS A MAJOR WOMEN'S CONFERENCE IN MEXICO CITY. IT WAS ATTENDED BY DELEGATES FROM 133 COUNTRIES.

THE CONFERENCE'S MAIN AIM WAS FOR WOMEN FROM ALL OVER THE WORLD TO BE RECOGNISED AS MEN'S EQUALS AND TO HAVE MORE OF A SAY IN SOCIETY.

A PLAN OF ACTION WAS DRAWN UP WITH A PARTICULAR FOCUS ON EDUCATION FOR WOMEN.

THERE WERE A LOT OF POSITIVE CHANGES IN THE YEARS THAT FOLLOWED, NOT LEAST IN THE WEST.

FAR MORE WOMEN STARTED STUDYING AT COLLEGES AND UNIVERSITIES.

IN MANY COUNTRIES PREGNANCY COULD NO LONGER BE USED AS A REASON FOR FIRING SOMEONE.

NURSERIES AND THE RIGHT TO MATERNITY LEAVE MEANT THAT WOMEN COULD HAVE PROPER CAREERS.

80 YEARS AFTER WOMEN STARTED MOBILISING
TO ACHIEVE SUFFRAGE, THE WORLD HAD ITS FIRST
FEMALE HEAD OF STATE.

HER NAME WAS SIRIMAVO
BANDARANAIKE AND SHE
BECAME PRIME MINISTER OF
SRI LANKA IN 1960.

THEN THERE WAS INDIRA
GANDHI, WHO BECAME
PRIME MINISTER OF INDIA
IN 1966.

GOLDA MEIR BECAME PRIME
MINISTER OF ISRAEL IN
1969.

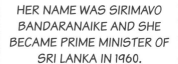

TODAY A NUMBER OF WOMEN HAVE BEEN HEADS OF STATE.

1974: ISABEL PÉRON IN ARGENTINA

1979: MARGARET THATCHER IN THE UNITED KINGDOM

1980: VIGDÍS FINNBOGADÓTTIR IN ICELAND

1981: GRO HARLEM BRUNDTLAND IN NORWAY

1988: BENAZIR BHUTTO IN PAKISTAN

1990: MARY ROBINSON IN IRELAND

1992: HANNA SUCHOCKA IN POLAND

1998: TANSU CILLER IN TURKEY

2005: ELLEN JOHNSON SIRLEAF IN LIBERIA

2005: ANGELA MERKEL IN GERMANY

2010: JULIA GILLARD IN AUSTRALIA

2011: DILMA ROUSSEFF IN BRAZIL

2011: HELLE THORNING-SCHMIDT IN DENMARK

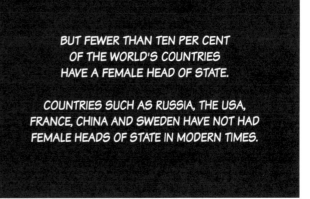

BUT FEWER THAN TEN PER CENT OF THE WORLD'S COUNTRIES HAVE A FEMALE HEAD OF STATE.

COUNTRIES SUCH AS RUSSIA, THE USA, FRANCE, CHINA AND SWEDEN HAVE NOT HAD FEMALE HEADS OF STATE IN MODERN TIMES.

FREE LOVE

SAME SEX RELATIONSHIPS HAVE ALWAYS EXISTED, BUT THEY HAVE NOT ALWAYS BEEN AS VISIBLE AS THEY ARE TODAY.

FOR CENTURIES HOMOSEXUALS HAD TO HIDE THEIR FEELINGS.

HOMOSEXUALITY WAS FORBIDDEN IN MOST COUNTRIES.

THESE LAWS WERE MOST OFTEN TO DO WITH MEN HAVING SEX WITH MEN.

IT WAS NOT DEEMED NECESSARY TO BRING WOMEN INTO IT.

WOMEN DON'T DO THAT SORT OF THING!

MOST PEOPLE DIDN'T REALISE THAT WOMEN COULD FALL IN LOVE WITH EACH OTHER.

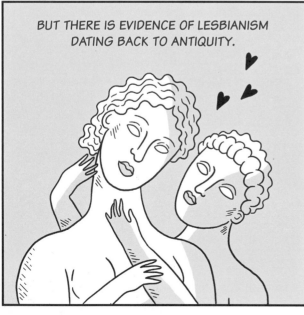

BUT THERE IS EVIDENCE OF LESBIANISM DATING BACK TO ANTIQUITY.

A POET CALLED SAPPHO LIVED ON THE GREEK ISLAND OF LESBOS.

SAPPHO
CA 630–612 BC

THE FIRST FEMALE
AUTHOR IN HISTORY.

SHE RAN A SCHOOL FOR GIRLS.

EVERY TIME ONE OF HER STUDENTS LEFT THE ISLAND, SAPPHO WOULD WRITE HER A BEAUTIFUL LOVE POEM.

YOU CAME AND I WAS CRAZY FOR YOU

AND YOU COOLED MY MIND THAT BURNED WITH LONGING

HER POEMS WERE SO INTENSE THAT THE NAME OF THE ISLAND, LESBOS, IS THE ORIGIN OF THE WORD "LESBIAN".

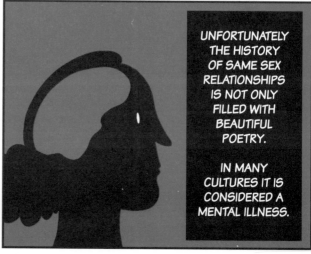

UNFORTUNATELY THE HISTORY OF SAME SEX RELATIONSHIPS IS NOT ONLY FILLED WITH BEAUTIFUL POETRY.

IN MANY CULTURES IT IS CONSIDERED A MENTAL ILLNESS.

PARENTS WHO DISCOVERED THAT THEIR CHILDREN WERE GAY HAD THEM LOCKED UP IN ASYLUMS.

IN RELIGIOUS ENVIRONMENTS THEY THOUGHT THE CONDITION COULD BE HEALED THROUGH PRAYER...

...OR EXORCISM.

IF THAT DIDN'T WORK, THE PERSON WAS TOLD SIMPLY TO STOP "PRACTISING".

JUST STOP!

WHICH MEANT THAT THEY HAD TO LIVE WITHOUT LOVE AND SEX.

DURING WWII THE NAZIS WANTED TO PUT AN END TO HOMOSEXUALITY ONCE AND FOR ALL.

THEY ARE A THREAT TO THE NATION'S MASCULINITY.

WE CAN'T LET THEM HAVE CHILDREN!

BEAUTIFUL, BLOND CHILDREN.

OVER A MILLION GAY GERMAN MEN WERE ON THE GESTAPO'S LISTS.

MANY OF THEM ENDED UP IN CONCENTRATION CAMPS, WHERE THEY DIED.

LESBIANS WERE NOT HUNTED DOWN IN THE SAME WAY. THE NAZIS THOUGHT IT WOULD BE EASIER TO FORCE THEM TO PRETEND TO BE STRAIGHT.

IN THE DECADES FOLLOWING THE WAR HOMOSEXUALS STARTED TO MOBILISE IN MANY WESTERN COUNTRIES.

AND DISCRIMINATION AGAINST HOMOSEXUALS WAS BANNED.

HERE COMES THE PC BRIGADE.

ONE OF THE MOST FAMOUS MOMENTS OF THE GAY LIBERATION MOVEMENT TOOK PLACE AT THE GAY CLUB STONEWALL IN NEW YORK.

ONE EVENING IN JUNE 1969 THE POLICE RAIDED THE CLUB FOR A "ROUTINE CHECK".

SINCE THIS HAPPENED QUITE OFTEN, THE PATRONS CLAIMED THAT THE POLICE WERE HARASSING THEM.

THAT EVENING THEY FOUGHT BACK. THERE WERE RIOTS BETWEEN THE HOMOSEXUAL COMMUNITY AND THE POLICE.

TRANSWOMEN ALSO TOOK AN ACTIVE PART IN THE FIGHT. THEY WOULD OFTEN EXPERIENCE THE POLICE BRUTALITY.

MARSHA P. JOHNSON (1945 - 1992)

PEOPLE'S EYES WERE OPENED TO THE OPPRESSION OF HOMOSEXUAL PEOPLE.

THIS PROMPTED THE PRIDE MOVEMENT.

TODAY HOMOSEXUAL COUPLES CAN GET MARRIED IN MANY COUNTRIES.

1989: DENMARK WAS THE FIRST COUNTRY IN THE WORLD TO INTRODUCE CIVIL PARTNERSHIPS.

2001: THE NETHERLANDS WAS THE FIRST COUNTRY TO INTRODUCE GAY MARRIAGE.

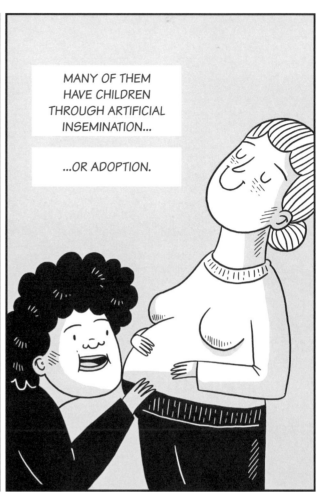

MANY OF THEM HAVE CHILDREN THROUGH ARTIFICIAL INSEMINATION...

...OR ADOPTION.

THEY CAN WORK IN THE MILITARY...

...AND AS PRIESTS IN SOME DENOMINATIONS.

BUT ALL OF THIS IS STILL A UTOPIA IN LARGE PARTS OF THE WORLD.

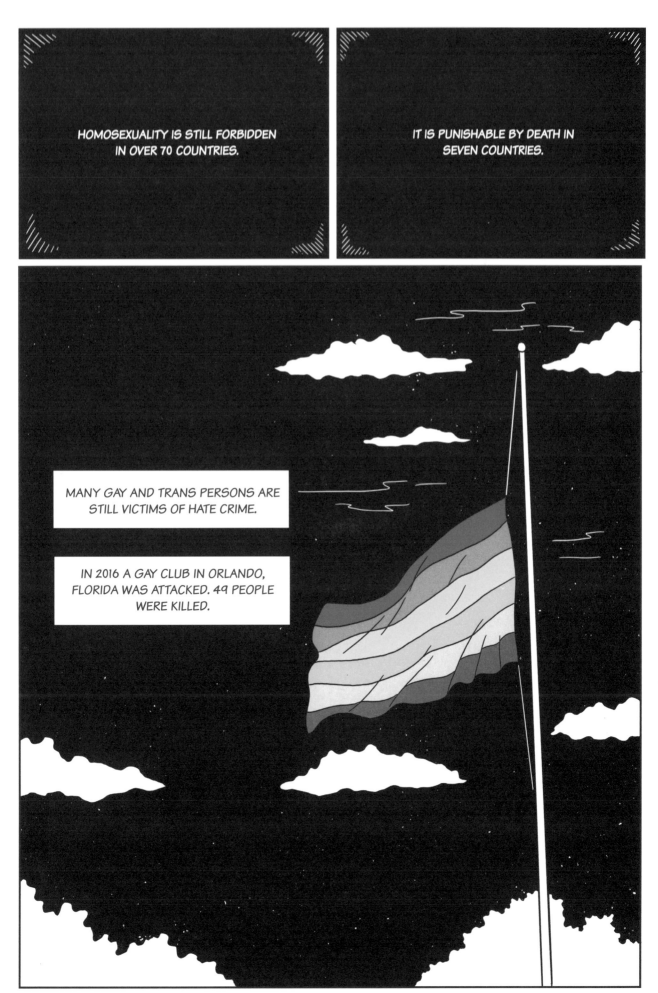

WHICH ONE OF YOU IS MALALA?

UNFORTUNATELY NOT EVERYTHING IS HEADING IN THE RIGHT DIRECTION.

IN SEVERAL COUNTRIES THERE IS LESS EQUALITY THAN BEFORE BECAUSE RELIGIOUS FANATICS HAVE SEIZED POWER.

AFGHANISTAN, 1965

AFGHANISTAN, 2015

FAR MORE GIRLS GO TO SCHOOL NOW THAN TEN YEARS AGO, BUT MANY STILL NEED TO FIGHT FOR THEIR RIGHT TO EDUCATION.

WHEN 17-YEAR-OLD MALALA YOUSAFZAI WAS AWARDED THE NOBEL PEACE PRIZE IN 2014, SHE WAS THE YOUNGEST LAUREATE EVER.

HER STORY BEGINS IN HER HOME TOWN, MINGORA, IN THE NORTHERN PART OF PAKISTAN.

HER FATHER, ZIAUDDIN, WHO IS A TEACHER AND POET, WANTED HIS DAUGHTER TO RECEIVE AN EDUCATION.

HE TAUGHT HER TO ALWAYS STAND UP TO INJUSTICE.

IN 2007 THE TALIBAN ADVANCED INTO THE VALLEY WHERE THE FAMILY LIVED.

THEY INTRODUCED STRICT LAWS AND RULES – AND GIRLS WERE NO LONGER ALLOWED TO GO TO SCHOOL.

THE TALIBAN DESTROYED AND BURNED DOWN THE GIRLS' SCHOOLS IN THE AREA.

SOON MALALA STARTED BLOGGING ABOUT HOW THINGS HAD CHANGED IN HER HOME TOWN.

SHE CRITICISED THE TALIBAN REGIME AND ARGUED IN FAVOUR OF GIRLS' RIGHT TO GO TO SCHOOL.

HER DIARY WAS PUBLISHED ANONYMOUSLY ON THE BBC'S WEBSITE.

WHEN THE TALIBAN DISCOVERED HER BLOG, THEY THREATENED HER.

ON DAY IN OCTOBER 2012 SHE WAS ON THE BUS HOME FROM A GIRLS' SCHOOL OUTSIDE OF THE TALIBAN'S AREA.

THE BUS WAS STOPPED BY A GROUP OF TALIBAN SOLDIERS.

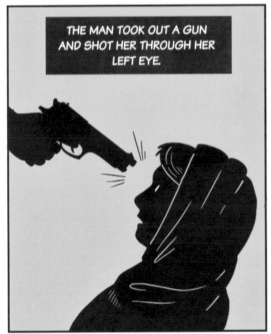

THE MAN TOOK OUT A GUN AND SHOT HER THROUGH HER LEFT EYE.

SEVERAL OF HER SCHOOL FRIENDS WERE ALSO HURT.

WE WARNED HER SEVERAL TIMES AND SAID SHE HAD TO STOP CRITICISING THE TALIBAN. WE ASKED HER TO FOLLOW THE PATH OF ISLAM.

SHE HAS BEEN INFECTED BY WESTERN IDEALS. WE WILL ATTACK ANYONE DEFYING THE TALIBAN.

MALALA UNDERWENT SURGERY IN THE UNITED KINGDOM.

SUDDENLY MALALA AND HER MESSAGE ABOUT EDUCATING WOMEN WERE HEARD BY THE WHOLE WORLD.

SHE WAS GIVEN A UK RESIDENCE PERMIT.

IN JANUARY 2013 SHE STARTED SCHOOL IN BIRMINGHAM.

A FEW MONTHS LATER – ON HER 16TH BIRTHDAY – SHE GAVE A SPEECH AT THE UN ON THE TOPIC OF A CHILD'S RIGHT TO AN EDUCATION.

"THE PEN IS MIGHTIER THAN THE SWORD." IT IS TRUE. A GUN CAN ONLY KILL, BUT A PEN CAN GIVE LIFE!

ON 10 OCTOBER 2014 IT WAS ANNOUNCED THAT MALALA WOULD RECEIVE THE NOBEL PEACE PRIZE.

THE WORLD PRESS HAD TO WAIT A FEW HOURS BEFORE MALALA WAS ABLE TO COMMENT ON THE JOYOUS NEWS.

SHE WANTED TO FINISH HER DAY AT SCHOOL FIRST.

THE AIM OF FEMINISM IS FOR ALL PEOPLE TO BE EQUAL REGARDLESS OF GENDER.

UNFORTUNATELY THIS IS JUST A DREAM FOR MANY PEOPLE AT PRESENT.

IN SOME COUNTRIES WOMEN HAVE ACHIEVED GREAT FREEDOM. IN OTHER COUNTRIES THERE IS VERY LITTLE EQUALITY.

IN RUSSIA THERE IS A LIST OF OVER 400 PROFESSIONS THAT WOMEN CANNOT HAVE.

FISHERMAN
BUS DRIVER
CARPENTER
DIVER

MANY GIRLS ARE MARRIED OFF AS CHILDREN.

IN SOME CULTURES GIRLS ARE CIRCUMCISED.

THIS IS A HORRENDOUS PRACTICE THAT INVOLVES REMOVING THE CLITORIS OR SEWING THE LABIA TOGETHER SO THAT THE GIRL CANNOT HAVE SEX.

IN SOME COUNTRIES WOMEN ARE CONSIDERED DIRTY WHEN THEY ARE MENSTRUATING. THEY ARE OFTEN LOCKED UP UNTIL THEY ARE "PURE" AGAIN.

MANY WOMEN EXPERIENCE OPPRESSION EVEN IN COUNTRIES THAT ARE PROUD OF THEIR EQUALITY.

WOMEN ARE SUBJECT TO HUMAN TRAFFICKING AND FORCED TO SELL THEIR BODIES.

WOMEN ARE RAPED AND ABUSED ALL OVER THE WORLD.

MANY WOMEN EXPERIENCE SEXUAL HARASSMENT AT SCHOOL OR AT WORK.

SLOWLY BUT SURELY WE ARE
MAKING PROGRESS.

WE NEED ONLY DARE TO BE HEARD.

This translation and production has taken place
with the financial support of NORLA

NORWEGIAN LITERATURE ABROAD

First published in Norway in 2018 by Cappelen Damm

First published in Great Britain in 2018 by
HOT KEY BOOKS
80–81 Wimpole St, London W1G 9RE
www.hotkeybooks.com

A CIP catalogue record for this book is available from the British Library.

ISBN: 978-1-4714-0812-0
also available as an ebook

1

Printed and bound in China

Hot Key Books is an imprint of Bonnier Zaffre Ltd,
a Bonnier Publishing company
www.bonnierpublishing.com